PRIMARY MATHEMATICS 3B

Third Edition

Primary Mathematics Project Team

Project Director
Dr Kho Tek Hong

Team Members
Chee Kum Hoong, Hector
Chip Wai Lung
Liang Hin Hoon
Lim Eng Tann
Lim Hui Cheng, Rosalind
Ng Hwee Wan
Ng Siew Lee

Curriculum Specialists
Cheong Ngan Peng, Christina
Ho Juan Beng

Curriculum Planning & Development Division
Ministry of Education, Singapore

FEDERAL PUBLICATIONS
An imprint of Times Media

D1504874

Published by
Times Media Private Limited
A member of the Times Publishing Group
Times Centre
1 New Industrial Road
Singapore 536196
E-mail: fps@tpl.com.sg
Online Book Store: http://www.timesone.com.sg/fpl

First published   1982
Second Edition 1993
Third Edition   1999
Reprinted   2000, 2001 (twice)

ISBN 981 01 8050 0

Printed by Times Offset (M) Sdn. Bhd

Illustrator
Paul Yong

ACKNOWLEDGEMENTS

The project team would like to record their thanks to the following:

* members of the Primary Mathematics Team who developed the first edition and second
  edition of the package

* members of the Steering Committee for the second edition of the package

* teachers who tested the materials in the package and provided useful insights and
  suggestions

* Educational Technology Division, for the design and production of the audio-visual
  components of the package

* all those who have helped in one way or another in the development and production of the
  package

PREFACE

The Primary Mathematics Package comprises textbooks, workbooks, teacher's guides and audio-visual materials.

The main feature of the package is the use of the **Concrete** ➡ **Pictorial** ➡ **Abstract** approach. The pupils are provided with the necessary learning experiences beginning with the concrete and pictorial stages, followed by the abstract stage to enable them to learn mathematics meaningfully. Like the previous editions of the package, this edition encourages active thinking processes, communication of mathematical ideas and problem solving.

This textbook is accompanied by two workbooks and a teacher's guide. It comprises 9 units. Each unit is divided into parts: **1**, **2**, . . . Each part starts with a meaningful situation for communication and is followed by specific learning tasks numbered 1, 2, . . . The sign Workbook Exercise is used to link the textbook to the workbook exercises.

Practice exercises are designed to provide the pupils with further practice after they have done the relevant workbook exercises. Review exercises and revision exercises are provided for cumulative reviews of concepts and skills. All the practice exercises, review exercises and revision exercises are optional exercises.

The colour patch ■ is used to invite active participation from the pupils and to facilitate oral discussion. The pupils are advised not to write on the colour patches.

CONTENTS

1 **Mental Calculation**

1	Addition	6
2	Subtraction	8
3	Multiplication	10
4	Division	11
	PRACTICE 1A	12
	PRACTICE 1B	13

2 **Length**

1	Metres and Centimetres	14
	PRACTICE 2A	18
2	Kilometres	19
	PRACTICE 2B	23

3 **Weight**

1	Kilograms and Grams	24
	PRACTICE 3A	28
2	More Word Problems	29
	PRACTICE 3B	33

Review A **34**

Review B **35**

4 **Capacity**

1	Litres and Millilitres	36
	PRACTICE 4A	42
	PRACTICE 4B	43

Review C **44**

Zoo Airport

5 **Graphs**
1   Bar Graphs   45

6 **Fractions**
1   Fraction of a Whole   51
     PRACTICE 6A   56
2   Equivalent Fractions   57
     PRACTICE 6B   62

Review D   **63**

7 **Time**
1   Hours and Minutes   65
     PRACTICE 7A   73
2   Other Units of Time   74
     PRACTICE 7B   76

Review E   **77**

8 **Geometry**
1   Angles   79
2   Right Angles   81

9 **Area and Perimeter**
1   Area   83
2   Perimeter   88
3   Area of a Rectangle   92
     PRACTICE 9A   94

Review F   **95**

Mental Calculation

1 Addition

Add 46 and 27.

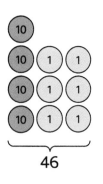

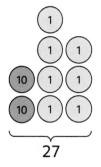

$$46 \xrightarrow{+20} 66 \xrightarrow{+7} 73$$

$$46 + 27 = \blacksquare$$

1. (a) $23 \xrightarrow{+10} \blacksquare \xrightarrow{+4} \blacksquare$

   $23 + 14 = \blacksquare$

   (b) $54 \xrightarrow{+30} \blacksquare \xrightarrow{+6} \blacksquare$

   $54 + 36 = \blacksquare$

   (c) $38 \xrightarrow{+40} \blacksquare \xrightarrow{+5} \blacksquare$

   $38 + 45 = \blacksquare$

2. (a) What number is 3 more than 68?
   (b) What number is 20 more than 94?

3. Add.
   (a) $43 + 30$ (b) $67 + 20$ (c) $85 + 50$
   (d) $72 + 5$ (e) $33 + 7$ (f) $64 + 8$
   (g) $36 + 23$ (h) $27 + 35$ (i) $55 + 26$

Workbook Exercise 1

4. Find the sum of 58 and 16.

   $58 + 16 = \blacksquare$

   $$58 + 16$$
   $$\diagup \diagdown$$
   $$2 \quad 14$$

   $58 + 2 = 60$
   $58 + 16 = 60 + 14$

5. Add.
   (a) $39 + 27$ (b) $58 + 34$ (c) $45 + 65$

Workbook Exercise 2

② Subtraction

Subtract 34 from 87.

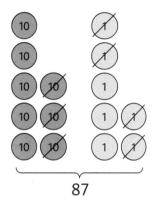

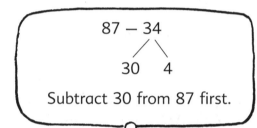

$$87 \xrightarrow{-30} 57 \xrightarrow{-4} 53$$

$$87 - 34 = \blacksquare$$

1. (a) $65 \xrightarrow{-10} \blacksquare \xrightarrow{-2} \blacksquare$

   $65 - 12 = \blacksquare$

   (b) $76 \xrightarrow{-40} \blacksquare \xrightarrow{-6} \blacksquare$

   $76 - 46 = \blacksquare$

   (c) $63 \xrightarrow{-20} \blacksquare \xrightarrow{-8} \blacksquare$

   $63 - 28 = \blacksquare$

2. (a) What number is 2 less than 51?
   (b) What number is 30 less than 76?

3. Subtract.
   (a) 70 − 30   (b) 95 − 70
   (c) 68 − 60   (d) 58 − 6
   (e) 83 − 3   (f) 47 − 9

4. Subtract.
   (a) 48 − 32   (b) 64 − 34
   (c) 85 − 59   (d) 56 − 24
   (e) 87 − 47   (f) 63 − 55

5. Find the difference between 90 and 18.

   90 − 18 = ▮

   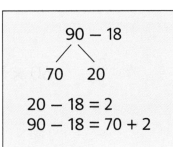

6. Subtract.
   (a) 30 − 28   (b) 60 − 56
   (c) 70 − 65   (d) 50 − 17
   (e) 40 − 29   (f) 80 − 58
   (g) 40 − 16   (h) 70 − 58
   (i) 90 − 39

Workbook Exercise 3

③ Multiplication

Multiply 3 tens by 4.

3 tens × 4 = 12 tens

30 × 4 = ■

1. (a) Multiply 6 tens by 5.   6 tens × 5 = ■ tens

60 × 5 = ■

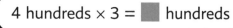

(b) Multiply 4 hundreds by 3.   4 hundreds × 3 = ■ hundreds

400 × 3 = ■

2. Multiply.
   (a) 8 × 7   (b) 80 × 7   (c) 800 × 7
   (d) 50 × 9   (e) 40 × 8   (f) 90 × 6
   (g) 600 × 3   (h) 300 × 5   (i) 700 × 4

Workbook Exercise 4

4 Division

Divide 6 tens by 3.

6 tens ÷ 3 = 2 tens

60 ÷ 3 = ■

1. (a) Divide 8 tens by 4.

8 tens ÷ 4 = ■ tens

80 ÷ 4 = ■

(b) Divide 6 hundreds by 2.

6 hundreds ÷ 2 = ■ hundreds

600 ÷ 2 = ■

2. Divide
   (a) 9 ÷ 3   (b) 90 ÷ 3   (c) 900 ÷ 3
   (d) 40 ÷ 2   (e) 360 ÷ 6   (f) 400 ÷ 10
   (g) 320 ÷ 8   (h) 2400 ÷ 4   (i) 1000 ÷ 5

Workbook Exercise 5

PRACTICE 1A

Find the value of each of the following:

	(a)	(b)	(c)
1.	65 + 28	34 + 66	18 + 84
2.	99 + 99	99 + 98	27 + 45
3.	78 − 45	90 − 56	90 − 85
4.	99 − 98	83 − 75	98 − 97
5.	4 × 30	50 × 8	200 × 9
6.	500 ÷ 5	600 ÷ 10	400 ÷ 2
7.	100 × 6	5 × 90	300 × 7
8.	160 ÷ 8	240 ÷ 3	810 ÷ 9
9.	6 × 100	40 × 6	500 × 5

10. (a) What number is 29 less than 84?
    (b) What number is 68 less than 310?
    (c) What number is 35 more than 475?
    (d) What number is 97 more than 5397?

11. There are 80 pages in one exercise book.
    How many pages are there in 6 exercise books?

12. A shopkeeper packed 200 onions equally into 5 bags.
    How many onions were there in each bag?

13. Mr Wu sold 70 buns on Friday.
    He sold 4 times as many buns on Sunday as on Friday.
    How many buns did he sell on Sunday?

PRACTICE 1B

Find the value of each of the following:

	(a)	(b)	(c)
1.	50 × 3	60 × 5	30 × 6
2.	40 ÷ 2	80 ÷ 4	600 ÷ 3
3.	6 × 90	7 × 400	300 × 8
4.	270 ÷ 9	320 ÷ 8	720 ÷ 9

5. Alice saves $50 a month.
    How much does she save in 8 months?

6. A cake shop sold 200 kaya buns.
    It sold 4 times as many kaya buns as chocolate buns.
    How many chocolate buns did it sell?

7. A fruit seller bought 9 boxes of pears.
    There were 40 pears in each box.
    How many pears did he buy altogether?

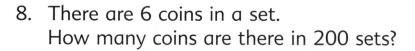

8. There are 6 coins in a set.
    How many coins are there in 200 sets?

9. Mr Fu packed 250 tomatoes into packets of 5 each.
    (a) How many packets of tomatoes were there?
    (b) He sold all the tomatoes at $2 a packet.
         How much money did he receive?

10. (a) Mr Lin bought 98 blue pens and 62 red pens. How
         many pens did he buy altogether?
    (b) He divided the pens equally into 8 boxes. How many
         pens were there in each box?

Length

1 Metres and Centimetres

Get a metre ruler and find out how long 1 metre is.

Estimate the length of the chalkboard in the classroom. Then check by measuring it with the metre ruler.

Is the length closer to 2 m or 3 m?

Estimate the height of the door in your classroom. Check by measuring.

Is the door 2 m high?

The **metre (m)** and **centimetre (cm)** are units of length.
1 m = 100 cm

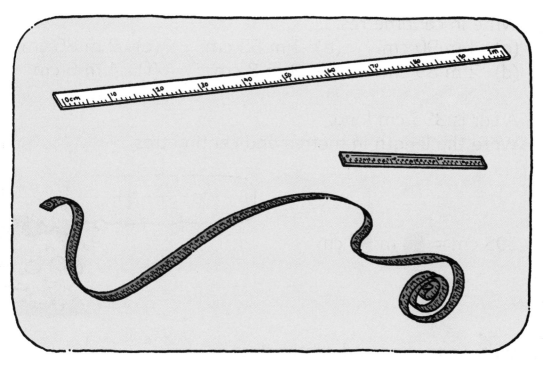

1. Ali's height is 1 m 25 cm.
    (a) 1 m 25 cm is ▮ cm more than 1 m.
    (b) 1 m 25 cm = ▮ cm

2. (a) Write 2 m in centimetres.
        2 m = ▮ cm
    (b) Write 300 cm in metres.
        300 cm = ▮ m

3. Walk 5 steps.
    Measure the distance in metres and centimetres.
    Then write the distance in centimetres.

4. Hashim's long jump result is 1 m 45 cm.
   Write the distance in centimetres.

   1 m 45 cm = 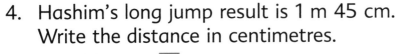 cm

5. Write in centimetres.
   (a) 1 m 90 cm   (b) 1 m 55 cm   (c) 2 m 86 cm
   (d) 2 m 89 cm   (e) 3 m 8 cm   (f) 4 m 6 cm

6. A car is 395 cm long.
   Write the length in metres and centimetres.

   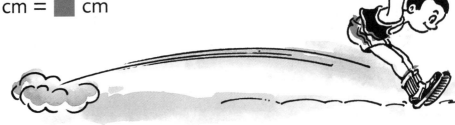

   300 cm = 3 m

   395 cm =  m   cm

7. Write in metres and centimetres.
   (a) 180 cm   (b) 195 cm   (c) 262 cm
   (d) 299 cm   (e) 304 cm   (f) 409 cm

8. The table shows the results of the shot put finals.

Name	Distance
Raju	1 m 89 cm
Rami	2 m 8 cm
Huamin	1 m 96 cm

   Arrange the distances in order. Begin with the shortest.

Workbook Exercise 6

9. Lily has a piece of red ribbon 3 m 40 cm long and a piece of yellow ribbon 1 m 85 cm long.

    (a) Find the total length of the ribbons.

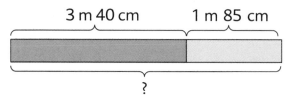

3 m 40 cm + 1 m 85 cm = ⬛ m ⬛ cm

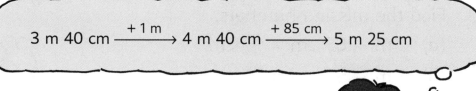

3 m 40 cm $\xrightarrow{+\,1\,m}$ 4 m 40 cm $\xrightarrow{+\,85\,cm}$ 5 m 25 cm

The total length of the ribbons is ⬛ m ⬛ cm.

    (b) How much longer is the red ribbon than the yellow ribbon?

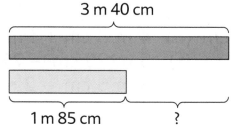

3 m 40 cm — 1 m 85 cm = ⬛ m ⬛ cm

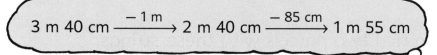

3 m 40 cm $\xrightarrow{-\,1\,m}$ 2 m 40 cm $\xrightarrow{-\,85\,cm}$ 1 m 55 cm

The red ribbon is ⬛ m ⬛ cm longer than the yellow ribbon.

Workbook Exercise 7

17

PRACTICE 2A

1. Write in centimetres.
    (a) 4 m
    (b) 1 m 40 cm
    (c) 2 m 25 cm
    (d) 3 m 95 cm
    (e) 4 m 5 cm
    (f) 9 m 9 cm

2. Write in metres and centimetres.
    (a) 120 cm
    (b) 225 cm
    (c) 309 cm
    (d) 618 cm
    (e) 963 cm
    (f) 405 cm

3. Find the missing numbers.

    (a) 1 m − 65 cm = ▊ cm
    (b) 1 m − 55 cm = ▊ cm
    (c) 2 m − 1 m 75 cm = ▊ cm
    (d) 2 m − 95 cm = ▊ m ▊ cm
    (e) 3 m − 2 m 92 cm = ▊ cm
    (f) 3 m 40 cm − 6 cm = ▊ m ▊ cm

4. Add or subtract in compound units.
    (a) 2 m 75 cm + 3 m
    (b) 3 m 4 cm + 65 cm
    (c) 1 m 26 cm + 2 m 65 cm
    (d) 4 m 8 cm + 1 m 95 cm
    (e) 5 m 85 cm − 5 m
    (f) 5 m 90 cm − 76 cm
    (g) 2 m 55 cm − 1 m 50 cm
    (h) 3 m 6 cm − 2 m 25 cm

5. Rahim is 1 m 60 cm tall.
    Raju is 16 cm shorter than Rahim.
    What is Raju's height?

6. Mr Chen tied two parcels with these strings.

1 m 80 cm   1 m 65 cm

What was the total length of the strings?

18

2 Kilometres

The **kilometre (km)**, metre (m) and centimetre (cm) are units of length.

1 km = 1000 m
1 m = 100 cm

A bus is about 10 m long,
The total length of 100 buses
is about 1 km.

We measure long distances
in kilometres.

ECP
1 km

1.
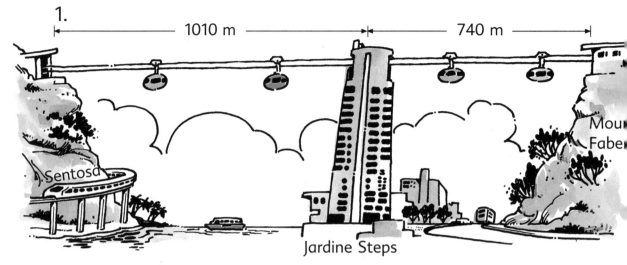

1010 m   740 m

Mou
Fabe

Sentosa

Jardine Steps

(a) The distance between Sentosa and Jardine Steps
is ☐ km ☐ m.

(b) The distance between Mount Faber and Sentosa
is ☐ km ☐ m.

2.
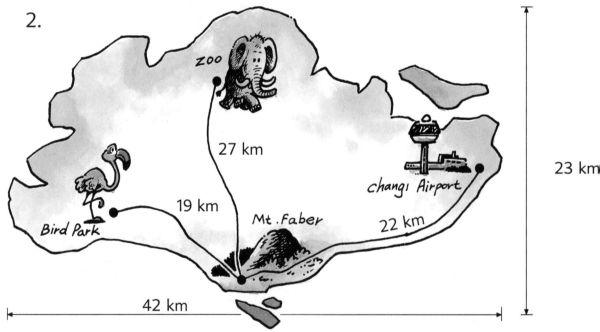

Zoo

27 km

23 km

Changi Airport

19 km

Mt. Faber

22 km

Bird Park

42 km

(a) The distance across Singapore is about ☐ km from west
to east.
It is about ☐ km from north to south.

(b) The distance from the Bird Park to Changi Airport is
about ☐ km.

3.

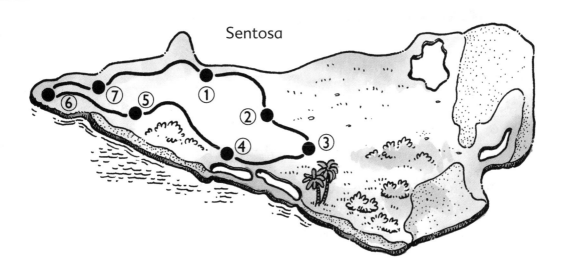

The total length of the Monorail route on Sentosa Island is about 6 km 100 m.
Write the length in metres.

6 km = 6000 m

4. The distance around a running track is 400 m.
Raju ran round the track 3 times.

He ran ▮ km ▮ m.

5. Write in metres.
   (a) 1 km 600 m   (b) 2 km 550 m   (c) 2 km 605 m
   (d) 3 km 85 m   (e) 3 km 20 m   (f) 4 km 5 m

6. Write in kilometres and metres.
   (a) 1830 m   (b) 2304 m   (c) 2780 m
   (d) 3096 m   (e) 3040 m   (f) 4009 m

Workbook Exercises 8 to 10

7.

| Army Camp | 2 km 450 m | Post Office | 1 km 850 m | Library |

Find the distance between the army camp and the library.

2 km 450 m + 1 km 850 m = ▮ km ▮ m

2 km 450 m $\xrightarrow{+1\ km}$ 3 km 450 m $\xrightarrow{+850\ m}$ 4 km 300 m

The distance between the army camp and the library is ▮ km ▮ m.

8.

| School A | 1 km 40 m | MRT Station | 920 m | School B |

Which school is nearer to the MRT station?
How much nearer?

1 km 40 m − 920 m = ▮ m

School B is ▮ m nearer to the MRT station.

Workbook Exercise 11

PRACTICE 2B

1. Write in metres.
   (a) 3 km   (b) 1 km 450 m   (c) 2 km 506 m
   (d) 2 km 60 m   (e) 3 km 78 m   (f) 4 km 9 m

2. Write in kilometres and metres.
   (a) 1680 m   (b) 1085 m   (c) 2204 m
   (d) 3090 m   (e) 3999 m   (f) 4001 m

3. Find the missing numbers.

   (a) 1 km − 800 m = ▮ m
   (b) 1 km − 600 m = ▮ m
   (c) 2 km − 1 km 45 m = ▮ m
   (d) 1 km − 40 m = ▮ m
   (e) 5 km − 4 km 940 m = ▮ m
   (f) 2 km − 275 m = ▮ km ▮ m

4. Add or subtract in compound units.
   (a) 2 km 650 m + 3 km
   (b) 3 km 460 m + 50 m
   (c) 3 km 300 m + 800 m
   (d) 4 km 700 m + 1 km 300 m
   (e) 5 km 950 m − 4 km
   (f) 4 km 820 m − 720 m
   (g) 6 km 25 m − 3 km 350 m
   (h) 5 km 40 m − 3 km 990 m

5. Find the distance between the gun boat
   and the lighthouse.

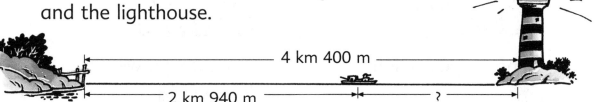

4 km 400 m

2 km 940 m   ?

23

Weight

1 ## Kilograms and Grams

The **kilogram (kg)** and **gram (g)** are units of weight.

1 kg = 1000 g

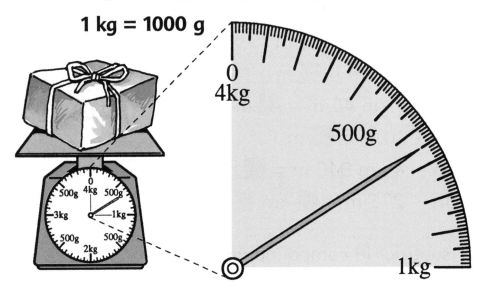

The parcel weighs 650 g.

The grapes weigh
█ g.

The papaya weighs
█ kg █ g.

1. Read the scales.

(a)

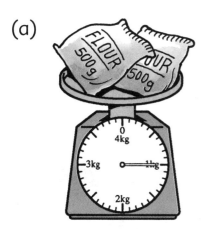

(b)

(c)

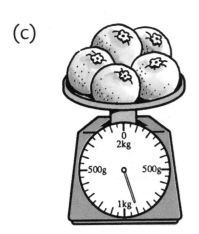

(d)

2. The potatoes weigh 2 kg 200 g.
   Write the weight in grams.

2 kg = 2000 g

3. Each book weighs 350 g.
   The total weight of 4 books
   is ▮ kg ▮ g.

Workbook Exercise 12

4. A bag of peanuts weighs 1 kg 850 g.
   How much more peanuts are needed to make up 2 kg?

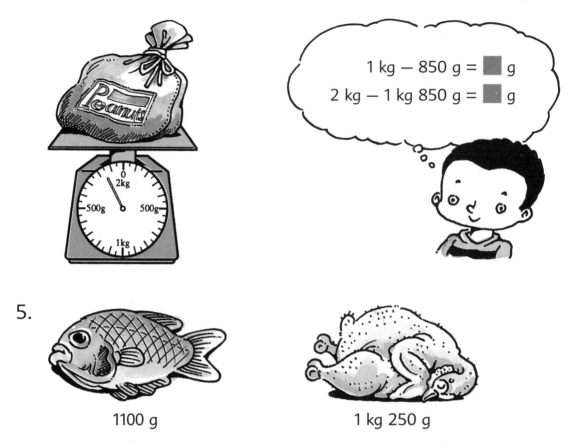

1 kg − 850 g = ▮ g
2 kg − 1 kg 850 g = ▮ g

5.

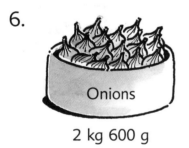

1100 g

1 kg 250 g

Which is heavier, the fish or the chicken?
How much heavier?

6.

Onions

2 kg 600 g

Tomatoes

1 kg 500 g

(a) What is the total weight of the onions and the
    tomatoes?
(b) What is the difference in weight between the onions
    and the tomatoes?

Workbook Exercises 13 & 14

7.

3 kg 80 g   1 kg 960 g

(a) Find the total weight of the watermelon and the bananas.

3 kg 80 g + 1 kg 960 g = ▮ kg ▮ g

3 kg 80 g $\xrightarrow{\text{+ 1 kg}}$ 4 kg 80 g $\xrightarrow{\text{+ 960 g}}$ 5 kg 40 g

The total weight is ▮ kg ▮ g.

(b) Find the difference in weight between the watermelon and the bananas.

3 kg 80 g − 1 kg 960 g = ▮ kg ▮ g

3 kg 80 g $\xrightarrow{\text{− 1 kg}}$ 2 kg 80 g $\xrightarrow{\text{− 960 g}}$ 1 kg 120 g

The difference in weight is ▮ kg ▮ g.

Workbook Exercise 15

PRACTICE 3A

1. Write in grams.
    (a) 1 kg 456 g
    (b) 2 kg 370 g
    (c) 3 kg 808 g
    (d) 2 kg 80 g
    (e) 1 kg 8 g
    (f) 4 kg 7 g

2. Write in kilograms and grams.
    (a) 2143 g
    (b) 1354 g
    (c) 3800 g
    (d) 2206 g
    (e) 3085 g
    (f) 4009 g

3. Find the missing numbers.
    (a) 1 kg − 395 g = ▉ g
    (b) 1 kg − 85 g = ▉ g
    (c) 3 kg − 2 kg 400 g = ▉ g
    (d) 5 kg − 4 kg 60 g = ▉ g
    (e) 1 kg − 540 g = ▉ g
    (f) 3 kg − 805 g = ▉ kg ▉ g

4. Add or subtract in compound units.
    (a) 3 kg 500 g + 2 kg
    (b) 4 kg 650 g + 450 g
    (c) 3 kg 100 g + 1 kg 900 g
    (d) 2 kg 50 g + 4 kg 70 g
    (e) 3 kg 10 g − 200 g
    (f) 4 kg 300 g − 1 kg 50 g
    (g) 4 kg 250 g − 1 kg 500 g
    (h) 5 kg − 2 kg 905 g

5. Lily weighed 25 kg 750 g two years ago.
    Now she weighs 32 kg.
    How much weight has she gained?

6. A jackfruit weighs 2 kg 990 g.
    A watermelon weighs 4 kg 200 g.
    (a) Find the total weight of the jackfruit and the
         watermelon.
    (b) Find the difference in weight between the jackfruit and
         the watermelon.

28

2 More Word Problems

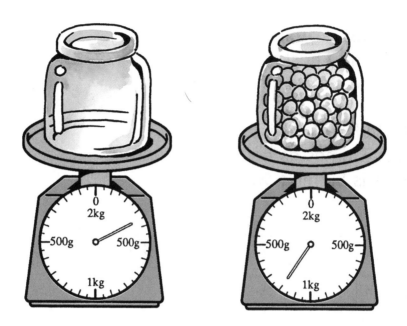

Weight of empty bottle	+	Weight of marbles	=	Total weight of bottle and marbles
(350 g)		(?)		(1 kg 200 g)

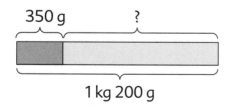

Weight of marbles = 1 kg 200 g − 350 g

= ▮ g

1. A bottle of sauce weighs 560 g.
   The empty bottle weighs 305 g.
   How many grams of sauce are there in the bottle?

2. A basket of fruits weighs 1 kg 60 g.
   The empty basket weighs 200 g.
   Find the weight of the fruits.

3. Mr Wu's weight is 57 kg.
   He is 3 times as heavy as Sumin.
   What is Sumin's weight?

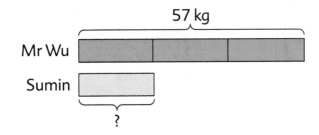

   3 units = 57 kg
   1 unit = ▨ kg
   Sumin's weight is ▨ kg.

4. A watermelon is 5 times as heavy as a papaya.
   If the papaya weighs 950 g, find the weight of the
   watermelon.

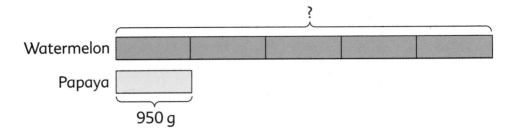

   1 unit = 950 g
   Weight of watermelon = 5 units
   $$= \blacksquare \text{ g}$$
   $$= \blacksquare \text{ kg } \blacksquare \text{ g}$$

5. John weighs 34 kg 600 g.
   He is 800 g heavier than David.
   What is David's weight?

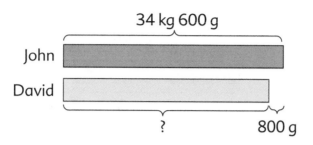

David's weight = 34 kg 600 g − 800 g
              = ▢ kg ▢ g

6. A goose weighs 3 kg 200 g.
   A duck weighs 1 kg 800 g.
   (a) What is the total weight of the goose and the duck?
   (b) What is the difference in weight between the goose
       and the duck?

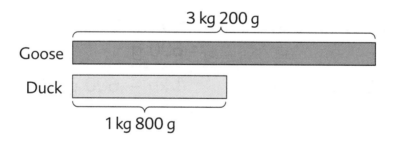

7. A durian weighs 2 kg 50 g.
   A jackfruit is 600 g heavier than the durian.
   (a) What is the weight of the jackfruit?
   (b) What is the total weight of the two fruits?

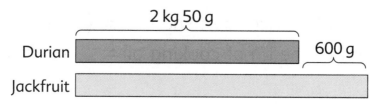

31

8. The total weight of a packet of flour and a packet of salt is
    2 kg 400 g.
    If the packet of flour weighs 1 kg 950 g, find the weight of
    the packet of salt.

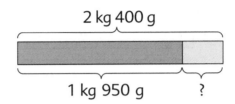

9. The total weight of a football and 10 tennis balls is 1 kg.
    If the weight of each tennis ball is 60 g, find the weight of
    the football.

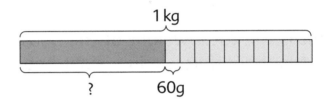

    Weight of 10 tennis balls = 60 × 10
                              = 600 g

    Weight of the football   = 1 kg − 600 g
                              = ▇ g

10. The total weight of a tin of cooking oil and 2 packets of
    sugar is 5 kg 50 g.
    If the weight of each packet of sugar is 2 kg, find the
    weight of the tin of cooking oil.

    Weight of 2 packets of sugar   = ▇ kg
    Weight of the tin of cooking oil = ▇ kg ▇ g

Workbook Exercise 16

PRACTICE 3B

1. Write in grams.
   (a) 5 kg   (b) 1 kg 950 g   (c) 1 kg 60 g
   (d) 2 kg 805 g   (e) 2 kg 5 g   (f) 3 kg 2 g

2. Write in kilograms and grams.
   (a) 1905 g   (b) 1055 g   (c) 2208 g
   (d) 3390 g   (e) 3599 g   (f) 5002 g

3. Add or subtract in compound units.
   (a) 2 kg 940 g + 300 g   (b) 3 kg 880 g + 1 kg 220 g
   (c) 4 kg − 1 kg 480 g   (d) 5 kg 20 g − 2 kg 450 g

4.

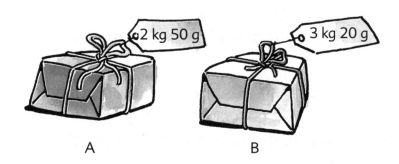

A   B

   (a) Find the total weight of the two parcels.
   (b) Find the difference in weight between the two parcels.

5. The total weight of Ali and Samy is 100 kg.
   If Ali's weight is 46 kg 540 g, find Samy's weight.

6. Raju's weight is 70 kg.
   He is 5 times as heavy as his son.
   Find the total weight of Raju and his son.

7. David weighs 39 kg.
   Hassan is twice as heavy as David.
   Mingli weighs 27 kg less than Hassan.
   What is Mingli's weight?

REVIEW A

Find the value of each of the following:

	(a)	(b)	(c)
1.	499 + 42	507 + 3593	3084 + 63
2.	750 − 145	1806 − 82	7009 − 5
3.	53 × 7	156 × 5	407 × 4
4.	87 ÷ 3	104 ÷ 8	324 ÷ 6

5. There are 24 boxes of chocolates in a carton.
   How many boxes of chocolates are there in 8 cartons?

6. 5 people shared $450 equally.
   How much money did each person receive?

7. Mrs Lin gave each of her friends 7 cup cakes.
   She gave away 140 cup cakes altogether.
   How many friends did she give the cup cakes to?

8. There are 8 boxes of yellow and green buttons.
   There are 46 buttons in each box.
   If there are 200 yellow buttons, how many green buttons
   are there?

9. There were 150 bulbs in a box.
   6 of them were broken.
   The rest were packed into boxes of 4 bulbs each.
   How many boxes of bulbs were there?

10. Mr Wang bought three boxes of oranges.
    There were 36 oranges in the first box.
    There were 54 oranges in each of the other two boxes.
    How many oranges did he buy?

REVIEW B

Find the missing numbers.

1. (a) 5 m = ■ cm   (b) 4 m 8 cm = ■ cm
   (c) 2 km 560 m = ■ m   (d) 3 km 5 m = ■ m
   (e) 1 kg 30 g = ■ g   (f) 2 kg 80 g = ■ g

2. (a) 208 cm = ■ m ■ cm
   (b) 320 cm = ■ m ■ cm
   (c) 1850 m = ■ km ■ m
   (d) 2004 m = ■ km ■ m
   (e) 3095 g = ■ kg ■ g
   (f) 4209 g = ■ kg ■ g

Add or subtract in compound units.

3. (a) 1 m 58 cm + 70 cm   (b) 2 m 95 cm + 2 m 45 cm
   (c) 3 m − 2 m 35 cm   (d) 4 m 5 cm − 1 m 85 cm

4. (a) 5 km 690 m + 520 m   (b) 7 km 960 m + 2 km 240 m
   (c) 9 km 420 m − 780 m   (d) 8 km 30 m − 3 km 480 m

5. (a) 4 kg 920 g + 125 g   (b) 3 kg 760 g + 4 kg 350 g
   (c) 6 kg − 4 kg 820 g   (d) 4 kg 25 g − 2 kg 230 g

6. (a) The total weight of the fruits is ■ g.
   (b) If the apple weighs 90 g, find the
       total weight of the two pears.
   (c) If the pears are of the same weight,
       find the weight of each pear.

Capacity

1 Litres and Millilitres

How much water is there in each of these beakers?

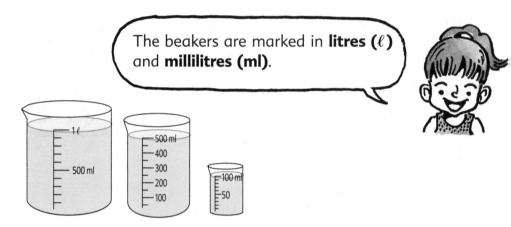

The beakers are marked in **litres (ℓ)** and **millilitres (ml)**.

What is the total amount of water in each set of beakers?

(a)

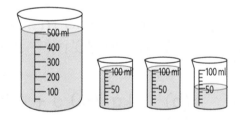

(b)

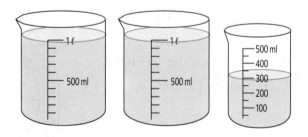

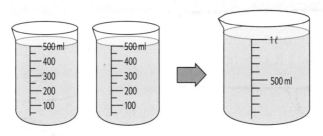

1 ℓ = 1000 ml

1. Get some paper cups.
   Find out how many paper cups you
   can fill with 1 litre of water.

2. Get a pail.
   Find out how much water the pail
   can hold.

3.

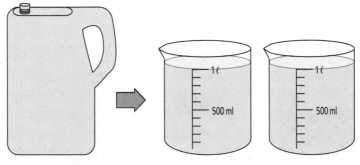

The bottle holds 2 litres of water.
Its **capacity** is ▮ litres.

Workbook Exercise 17

The capacity of a container is the amount it can hold.

We measure capacity in litres and millilitres.

4. (a)

The capacity of the mug is ⬛ ml.

(b)

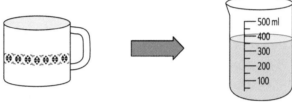

The capacity of the bottle is ⬛ ml.

(c)

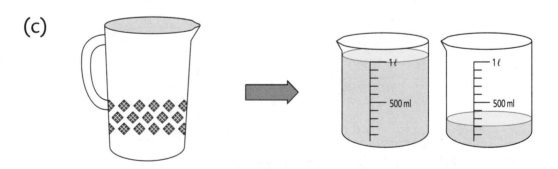

The capacity of the jug is ⬛ ℓ ⬛ ml.

5. (a) Get a bottle which holds less than 1 litre of water. Estimate and then measure its capacity.
   (b) Get a bottle which holds more than 1 litre of water. Estimate and then measure its capacity.

Workbook Exercises 18 & 19

6. Find the total amount of water in these two beakers.

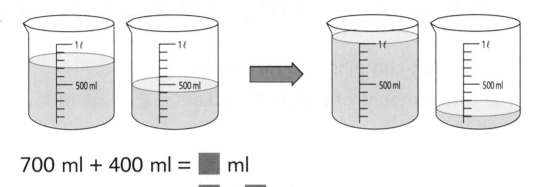

700 ml + 400 ml = ▇ ml

= ▇ ℓ ▇ ml

7. Write 1500 ml in litres and millilitres.

1500 ml = ▇ ℓ ▇ ml

8. Write in litres and millilitres.
   (a) 1200 ml   (b) 2500 ml   (c) 2050 ml
   (d) 1005 ml   (e) 3400 ml   (f) 3105 ml

9. (a) Write 2 ℓ in millilitres.
      2 ℓ = ▇ ml
   (b) Write 2 ℓ 350 ml in millilitres.
      2 ℓ 350 ml = ▇ ml

10. Write in millilitres.
    (a) 1 ℓ 800 ml   (b) 1 ℓ 80 ml   (c) 1 ℓ 8 ml
    (d) 3 ℓ 25 ml   (e) 2 ℓ 5 ml   (f) 3 ℓ 500 ml

11.

Each packet contains 250 ml of milk.

The total amount of milk in 5 packets is ▇ ℓ ▇ ml.

12.

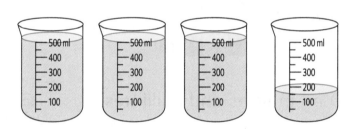

How many millilitres more water are needed to make up 2 litres?

13.

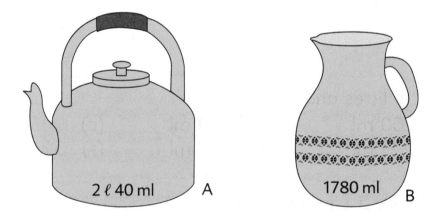

Which container can hold more water?
How much more?

Workbook Exercises 20 & 21 >

14.

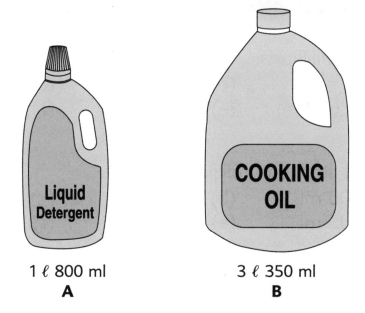

Liquid Detergent
1 ℓ 800 ml
A

COOKING OIL
3 ℓ 350 ml
B

(a) Find the total capacity of the two containers.

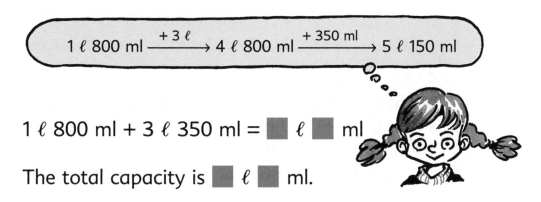

$$1 \ell\ 800\ \text{ml} \xrightarrow{\ +\,3\,\ell\ } 4\ \ell\ 800\ \text{ml} \xrightarrow{\ +\,350\ \text{ml}\ } 5\ \ell\ 150\ \text{ml}$$

1 ℓ 800 ml + 3 ℓ 350 ml = ▢ ℓ ▢ ml

The total capacity is ▢ ℓ ▢ ml.

(b) Find the difference in capacity between the two containers.

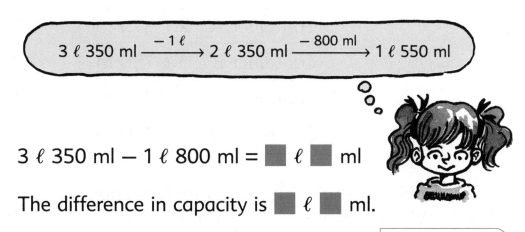

$$3 \ell\ 350\ \text{ml} \xrightarrow{\ -\,1\,\ell\ } 2\ \ell\ 350\ \text{ml} \xrightarrow{\ -\,800\ \text{ml}\ } 1\ \ell\ 550\ \text{ml}$$

3 ℓ 350 ml − 1 ℓ 800 ml = ▢ ℓ ▢ ml

The difference in capacity is ▢ ℓ ▢ ml.

Workbook Exercises 22 & 23

PRACTICE 4A

1. Write in millilitres.
   (a) 3 ℓ
   (b) 1 ℓ 200 ml
   (c) 2 ℓ 55 ml
   (d) 2 ℓ 650 ml
   (e) 3 ℓ 65 ml
   (f) 4 ℓ 5 ml

2. Write in litres and millilitres.
   (a) 5000 ml
   (b) 1600 ml
   (c) 2250 ml
   (d) 3205 ml
   (e) 2074 ml
   (f) 1009 ml

3. Circle the correct answer.
   (a) 1 ℓ is more than/equal to/less than 980 ml.
   (b) 2 ℓ 50 ml is more than/equal to/less than 2050 ml.
   (c) 4 ℓ 8 ml is more than/equal to/less than 4800 ml.

4. Add or subtract.
   (a) 1 ℓ 500 ml + 500 ml
   (b) 2 ℓ 800 ml + 1 ℓ 200 ml
   (c) 3 ℓ 300 ml + 750 ml
   (d) 5 ℓ 900 ml + 3 ℓ 240 ml
   (e) 2 ℓ 800 ml − 1 ℓ 780 ml
   (f) 4 ℓ − 1 ℓ 850 ml
   (g) 4 ℓ 80 ml − 1 ℓ 360 ml
   (h) 6 ℓ 5 ml − 2 ℓ 80 ml

5. The table shows the capacities of four containers.

Container A	2 ℓ 375 ml
Container B	1 ℓ 750 ml
Container C	1755 ml
Container D	2150 ml

   (a) Which container has the greatest capacity?
   (b) Which container has the smallest capacity?
   (c) What is the total capacity of the four containers?

PRACTICE 4B

1. The capacity of Container A is 2 ℓ 650 ml.
   The capacity of Container B is 5 ℓ 300 ml.
   (a) What is the total capacity of the two containers?
   (b) How much more water can Container B hold than
       Container A?

2. Container X holds 2 ℓ 800 ml of water.
   Container Y holds 1 ℓ 600 ml more water than Container X.
   How much water does Container Y hold?

3. Mrs Chen fills a container with 9 bottles of orange juice.
   Each bottle contains 2 litres of orange juice.
   What is the capacity of the container?

4. The capacity of a pail is 6 litres.
   5 pails of water are needed to fill up a tank.
   What is the capacity of the tank?

5. The capacity of a container is 24 litres.
   How many pails of water are needed to fill up the container
   if the capacity of the pail is 3 litres?

6. The capacity of a container is 8 litres.
   It contains 4 ℓ 650 ml of water.
   How much more water is needed to fill up the container?

7. Mr Li bought 6 tins of paint.
   Each tin contained 3 litres of paint.
   He had 2 ℓ 400 ml of paint left after painting his house.
   How much paint did he use?

REVIEW C

Find the value of each of the following:

	(a)	(b)	(c)
1.	895 + 5037	6409 + 399	2846 + 754
2.	1436 − 437	3002 − 78	5362 − 26
3.	77 × 4	73 × 9	123 × 5
4.	900 ÷ 2	408 ÷ 3	518 ÷ 8

5. Mr Chen received $504 for selling pens at $8 each.
   How many pens did he sell?

6. Mr Wu paid $628 for a television set and $1485 for
   a computer.
   He had $515 left.
   How much money did he have at first?

7. Mrs Chen bought 4 boxes of cookies.
   There were 12 chocolate cookies and 8 peanut cookies in
   each box.
   How many cookies were there altogether?

8. Mr Li sold 337 packets of biscuits last month.
   He sold 299 more packets this month than last month.
   How many packets of biscuits did he sell in the two
   months?

9. Sally bought 200 eggs to make cakes.
   She used 8 eggs to make each cake.
   (a) How many cakes did she make?
   (b) If she sold all the cakes at $10 each, how much money
       would she receive?

Graphs

1 Bar Graphs

This picture graph shows the number of fish caught by four boys.

Minghua	Rohan	Samy	Yonghua
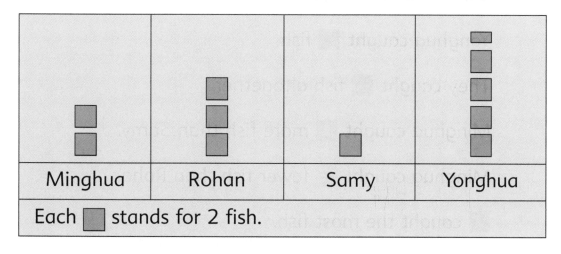

How many fish did each boy catch?

This **bar graph** shows the same information.

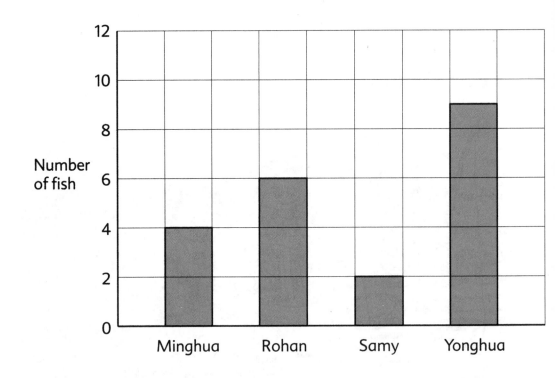

Minghua caught ■ fish.

Rohan caught ■ fish.

Samy caught ■ fish.

Yonghua caught ■ fish.

They caught ■ fish altogether.

Minghua caught ■ more fish than Samy.

Minghua caught ■ fewer fish than Rohan.

■ caught the most fish.

■ caught the fewest fish.

1. This bar graph shows Rahim's examination results for four subjects.

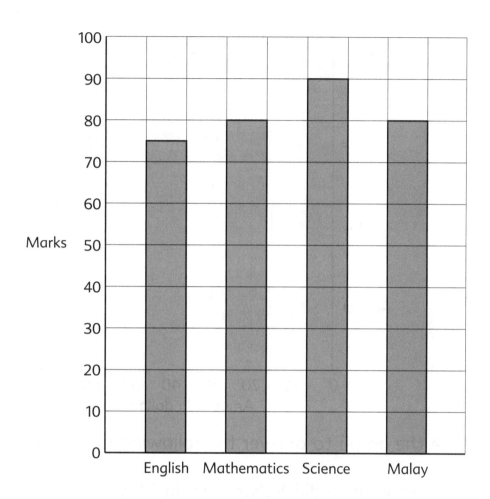

Use the graph to complete the following.

(a) Rahim scored 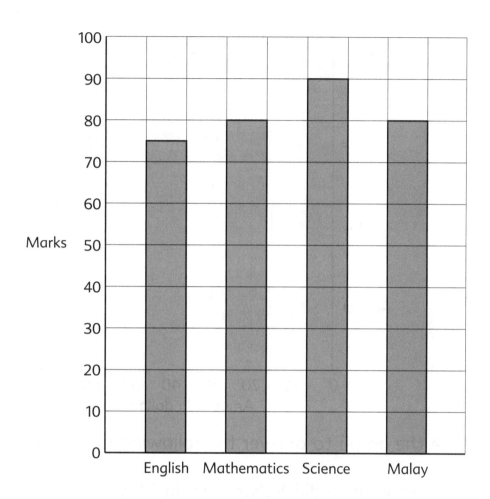 marks in English.

(b) He scored ▮ marks in Mathematics.

(c) He scored ▮ more marks in Mathematics than in English.

(d) He had the same score in ▮ and ▮.

(e) He scored 10 more marks in ▮ than in Mathematics.

(f) His highest score was in ▮.

(g) His lowest score was in ▮.

2. This bar graph shows Sulian's savings for four months.

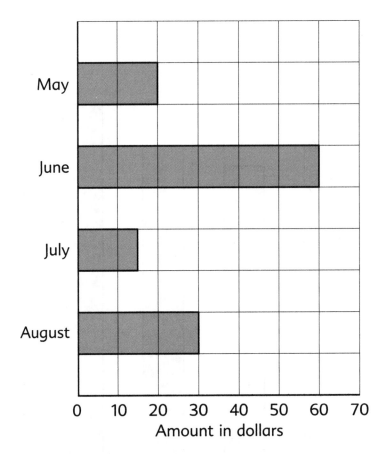

Amount in dollars

Use the graph to answer the following questions.

(a) How much did Sulian save in May?

(b) How much more did she save in June than in May?

(c) In which month did she save $15?

(d) In which month did she save the most?

(e) In which month did she save twice as much as in August?

(f) What was her total savings for the four months?

Workbook Exercise 24

3. This bar graph shows the number of books read by five children in a year.

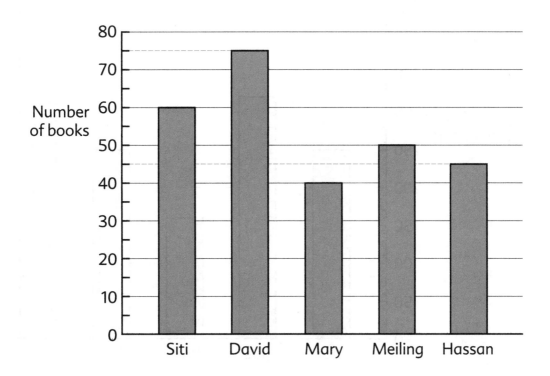

Use the graph to answer the following questions.

(a) How many books did Siti read?

(b) How many books did David read?

(c) How many more books did David read than Meiling?

(d) Who read 5 fewer books than Meiling?

(e) Who read the most books?

(f) Who read the fewest books?

4. This bar graph shows the number of people who visited a book fair from Monday to Friday.

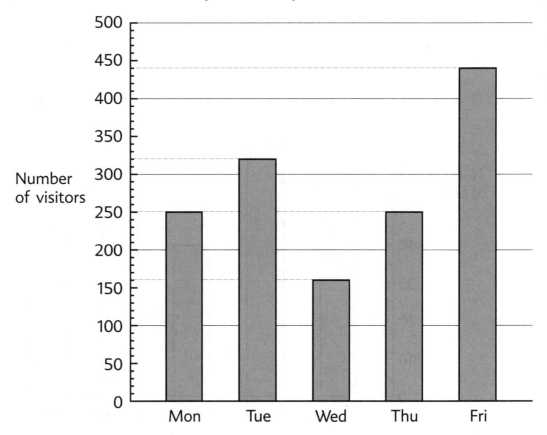

Use the graph to answer the following questions.

(a) How many people visited the book fair on Tuesday?

(b) How many more people visited the book fair on Friday than on Thursday?

(c) On which day was the number of visitors the smallest?

(d) On which day were there as many visitors as on Monday?

(e) On which day were there twice as many visitors as on Wednesday?

(f) If there were 200 adults on Tuesday, how many children were there?

Workbook Exercise 25

6

Fractions

Fraction of a Whole

a whole   2 fifths   3 fifths

How many fifths are there in a whole?

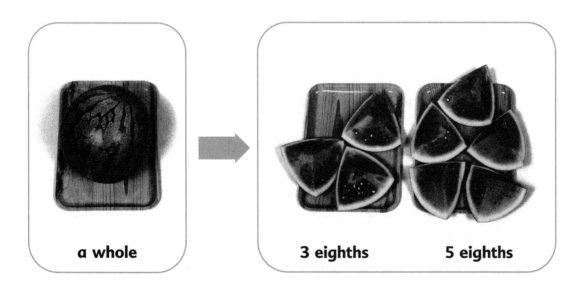

a whole   3 eighths   5 eighths

How many eighths are there in a whole?

1.

(a) $\frac{2}{5}$ of the bar is shaded.

   $\frac{2}{5}$ is ■ out of the ■ equal parts.

   $\frac{2}{5}$ = ■ fifths

(b) $\frac{3}{5}$ of the bar is **not** shaded.

   $\frac{3}{5}$ is ■ out of the ■ equal parts.

   $\frac{3}{5}$ = ■ fifths

(c) 1 whole = ■ fifths

   $1 = \dfrac{■}{5}$

2.

(a) $\frac{3}{8}$ of the bar is shaded.

   ■ of the bar is **not** shaded.

(b) 1 whole = ■ eighths

   $1 = \dfrac{■}{8}$

(c) $\frac{3}{8}$ and ■ make 1 whole.

3. What fraction of each shape is shaded?

(a)

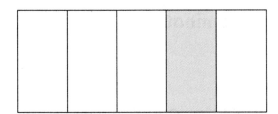

(b)

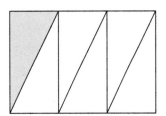

(c)

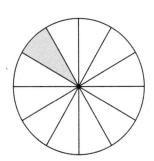

(d)

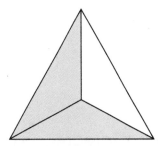

(e)

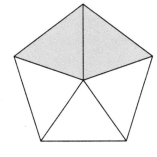

(f)

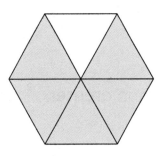

(g)

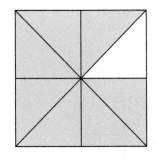

(h)

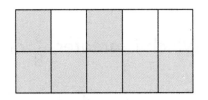

Workbook Exercises 26 to 28

4.

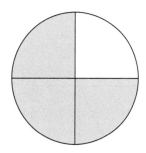

In the fraction $\frac{3}{4}$, 3 is the numerator and 4 is the denominator.

Name the numerator and denominator of each of these fractions.

(a) $\frac{2}{5}$ (b) $\frac{4}{10}$ (c) $\frac{6}{7}$ (d) $\frac{6}{9}$

5. Which is greater, $\frac{1}{5}$ or $\frac{1}{3}$?

6. Which is greater, $\frac{3}{4}$ or $\frac{3}{5}$?

7. Which is greater, $\frac{3}{8}$ or $\frac{5}{8}$?

It is easy to compare fractions when they have a common numerator or a common denominator.

8.

 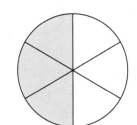 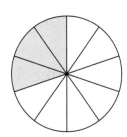

The fractions $\frac{3}{5}$, $\frac{3}{6}$ and $\frac{3}{10}$ have a common numerator.

■ is the smallest fraction.

■ is the greatest fraction.

9.

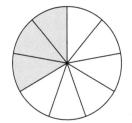 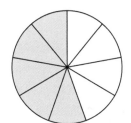 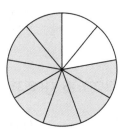

The fractions $\frac{3}{9}$, $\frac{5}{9}$ and $\frac{7}{9}$ have a common denominator.

■ is the smallest fraction.

■ is the greatest fraction.

10. Arrange the fractions in order.
Begin with the smallest.

(a) $\frac{1}{5}$, $\frac{1}{7}$, $\frac{1}{3}$

(b) $\frac{2}{7}$, $\frac{2}{3}$, $\frac{2}{9}$

(c) $\frac{5}{8}$, $\frac{7}{8}$, $\frac{4}{8}$

(d) $\frac{5}{12}$, $\frac{9}{12}$, $\frac{4}{12}$

Workbook Exercises 29 & 30

PRACTICE 6A

1. Find the missing numbers.

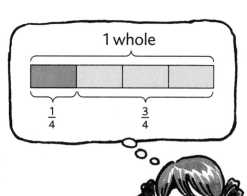

(a) $\frac{1}{4}$ and ■ make 1 whole.

(b) $\frac{3}{10}$ and ■ make 1 whole.

(c) $\frac{7}{12}$ and ■ make 1 whole.

2. Name the numerator of each fraction.

(a) $\frac{2}{3}$ (b) $\frac{6}{10}$ (c) $\frac{9}{12}$

3. Name the denominator of each fraction.

(a) $\frac{5}{8}$ (b) $\frac{4}{9}$ (c) $\frac{7}{10}$

4. Which fraction is greater?

(a) $\frac{2}{5}$ or $\frac{4}{5}$ (b) $\frac{1}{4}$ or $\frac{1}{6}$ (c) $\frac{3}{8}$ or $\frac{3}{5}$

5. Which fraction is smaller?

(a) $\frac{7}{10}$ or $\frac{3}{10}$ (b) $\frac{1}{8}$ or $\frac{1}{10}$ (c) $\frac{2}{9}$ or $\frac{2}{3}$

6. Which is the greatest fraction?

(a) $\frac{4}{7}$, $\frac{1}{7}$, $\frac{5}{7}$ (b) $\frac{1}{4}$, $\frac{1}{2}$, $\frac{1}{5}$

7. Which is the smallest fraction?

(a) $\frac{5}{6}$, $\frac{1}{6}$, $\frac{4}{6}$ (b) $\frac{3}{9}$, $\frac{3}{5}$, $\frac{3}{10}$

② Equivalent Fractions

Fold a piece of paper into 2 equal parts.
Shade 1 part.

1 out of
2 equal parts

$\frac{1}{2}$ of the paper is shaded.

Fold the paper again.

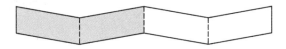

2 out of
4 equal parts

$\frac{2}{4}$ of the paper is shaded.

Fold the paper again.

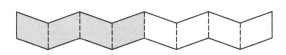

4 out of
8 equal parts

$\frac{4}{8}$ of the paper is shaded.

The fractions $\frac{1}{2}$, $\frac{2}{4}$ and $\frac{4}{8}$ have different numerators and denominators.
But they are equal.

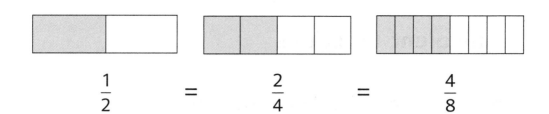

$$\frac{1}{2} \quad = \quad \frac{2}{4} \quad = \quad \frac{4}{8}$$

$\frac{1}{2}$, $\frac{2}{4}$ and $\frac{4}{8}$ are **equivalent fractions**.

Name some more equivalent fractions of $\frac{1}{2}$.

$\frac{2}{4}$ and $\frac{4}{8}$ are different ways of writing $\frac{1}{2}$.

1.

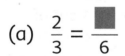

$\frac{2}{3}$ of the bar is shaded.

(a) $\frac{2}{3} = \frac{\blacksquare}{6}$

(b) $\frac{2}{3} = \frac{\blacksquare}{9}$

(c) $\frac{2}{3} = \frac{\blacksquare}{12}$

(d) Name some more equivalent fractions of $\frac{2}{3}$.

2. What are the missing numerators and denominators?

(a)

 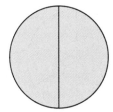  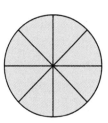

$$1 \quad = \quad \frac{\blacksquare}{2} \quad = \quad \frac{3}{\blacksquare} \quad = \quad \frac{\blacksquare}{\blacksquare}$$

(b)

 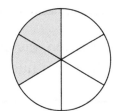 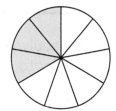 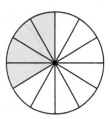

$$\frac{1}{3} \quad = \quad \frac{\blacksquare}{6} \quad = \quad \frac{3}{\blacksquare} \quad = \quad \frac{\blacksquare}{\blacksquare}$$

To find an equivalent fraction, multiply the numerator and denominator by the same number.

$$\frac{1}{3} \overset{\times 2}{\underset{\times 2}{=}} \frac{\blacksquare}{6} \qquad \frac{1}{3} \overset{\times 3}{\underset{\times 3}{=}} \frac{3}{\blacksquare}$$

3. Find the missing numerator or denominator.

(a) $\dfrac{1}{4} = \dfrac{\blacksquare}{12}$ (b) $\dfrac{2}{3} = \dfrac{\blacksquare}{9}$ (c) $\dfrac{1}{5} = \dfrac{\blacksquare}{10}$

(d) $\dfrac{1}{6} = \dfrac{3}{\blacksquare}$ (e) $\dfrac{3}{5} = \dfrac{6}{\blacksquare}$ (f) $\dfrac{3}{4} = \dfrac{6}{\blacksquare}$

Workbook Exercises 31 & 32

4. What are the missing numerators and denominators?

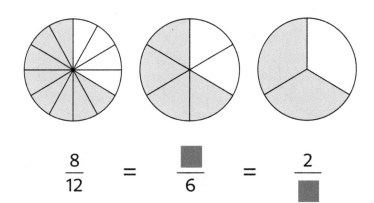

$$\frac{8}{12} \quad = \quad \frac{\boxed{}}{6} \quad = \quad \frac{2}{\boxed{}}$$

To find an equivalent fraction, divide the numerator and denominator by the same number.

$$\frac{8}{12} \overset{\div 2}{\underset{\div 2}{=}} \frac{\boxed{}}{6} \qquad \frac{8}{12} \overset{\div 4}{\underset{\div 4}{=}} \frac{2}{\boxed{}}$$

5. Find the missing numerator or denominator.

(a) $\frac{8}{10} = \frac{\boxed{}}{5}$

(b) $\frac{4}{8} = \frac{\boxed{}}{2}$

(c) $\frac{6}{9} = \frac{\boxed{}}{3}$

(d) $\frac{6}{9} = \frac{2}{\boxed{}}$

(e) $\frac{9}{12} = \frac{3}{\boxed{}}$

(f) $\frac{10}{12} = \frac{5}{\boxed{}}$

Workbook Exercise 33

6. Complete the following equivalent fractions of $\frac{6}{12}$.

$$\frac{6}{12} = \frac{3}{\boxed{}} \qquad \frac{6}{12} = \frac{2}{\boxed{}} \qquad \frac{6}{12} = \frac{1}{\boxed{}}$$

The simplest equivalent fraction of $\frac{6}{12}$ is $\frac{\boxed{}}{\boxed{}}$.

7. Express each of the following fractions in its simplest form.

(a) $\frac{2}{4}$ (b) $\frac{6}{8}$ (c) $\frac{5}{10}$ (d) $\frac{3}{9}$

(e) $\frac{4}{12}$ (f) $\frac{4}{6}$ (g) $\frac{10}{12}$ (h) $\frac{6}{10}$

Workbook Exercise 34

8. Which is greater, $\frac{3}{4}$ or $\frac{5}{8}$?

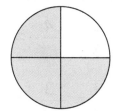
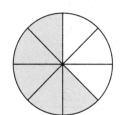

$$\frac{3}{4} = \frac{\blacksquare}{8}$$

9. Which is greater, $\frac{2}{5}$ or $\frac{7}{10}$?

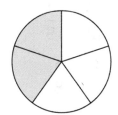
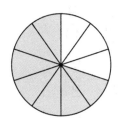

$$\frac{2}{5} = \frac{\blacksquare}{10}$$

10. Which fraction is greater?

(a) $\frac{2}{3}$, $\frac{5}{6}$ (b) $\frac{3}{8}$, $\frac{1}{2}$ (c) $\frac{3}{5}$, $\frac{4}{7}$

11. Which fraction is smaller?

(a) $\frac{4}{5}$, $\frac{7}{10}$ (b) $\frac{11}{12}$, $\frac{5}{6}$ (c) $\frac{2}{3}$, $\frac{3}{5}$

12. Arrange the fractions in order, beginning with the smallest.

(a) $\frac{5}{8}$, $\frac{1}{2}$, $\frac{3}{4}$ (b) $\frac{3}{10}$, $\frac{3}{5}$, $\frac{2}{5}$

Workbook Exercise 35

PRACTICE 6B

1. Find the missing numerator in each of the following:

   (a) $\dfrac{1}{4} = \dfrac{\blacksquare}{8}$

   (b) $\dfrac{3}{5} = \dfrac{\blacksquare}{15}$

   (c) $\dfrac{1}{3} = \dfrac{\blacksquare}{6} = \dfrac{\blacksquare}{9}$

   (d) $\dfrac{4}{10} = \dfrac{\blacksquare}{5}$

   (e) $\dfrac{6}{9} = \dfrac{\blacksquare}{3}$

   (f) $\dfrac{1}{2} = \dfrac{\blacksquare}{4} = \dfrac{\blacksquare}{6}$

2. Find the missing denominator in each of the following:

   (a) $\dfrac{2}{5} = \dfrac{4}{\blacksquare}$

   (b) $\dfrac{3}{4} = \dfrac{9}{\blacksquare}$

   (c) $\dfrac{2}{3} = \dfrac{4}{\blacksquare} = \dfrac{6}{\blacksquare}$

   (d) $\dfrac{6}{12} = \dfrac{1}{\blacksquare}$

   (e) $\dfrac{6}{8} = \dfrac{3}{\blacksquare}$

   (f) $\dfrac{1}{2} = \dfrac{3}{\blacksquare} = \dfrac{5}{\blacksquare}$

3. Ring the greater fraction.

   (a) $\dfrac{3}{10}, \quad \dfrac{7}{10}$

   (b) $\dfrac{5}{6}, \quad \dfrac{9}{12}$

   (c) $\dfrac{10}{12}, \quad \dfrac{4}{5}$

   (d) $\dfrac{1}{2}, \quad \dfrac{5}{6}$

   (e) $\dfrac{3}{4}, \quad \dfrac{2}{3}$

   (f) $\dfrac{3}{5}, \quad \dfrac{5}{8}$

4. Arrange the fractions in order, beginning with the smallest fraction.

   (a) $\dfrac{3}{7}, \quad \dfrac{1}{7}, \quad \dfrac{5}{7}$

   (b) $\dfrac{1}{5}, \quad \dfrac{1}{2}, \quad \dfrac{1}{10}$

   (c) $\dfrac{2}{3}, \quad \dfrac{1}{2}, \quad \dfrac{5}{6}$

   (d) $\dfrac{2}{3}, \quad \dfrac{1}{4}, \quad \dfrac{5}{12}$

5. Meiling ate $\dfrac{2}{6}$ of a pie.

   Suchen ate $\dfrac{1}{2}$ of the pie.

   Who ate a bigger portion of the pie?

REVIEW D

1. Write the numbers.
    (a) Nine thousand, two hundred and ten
    (b) Four thousand and sixty

2. Write the numbers in words.
    (a) 6204   (b) 3540   (c) 5028

3. What number is 100 less than 4000?

4. Write the numbers in order, beginning with the smallest.
    (a) 4104,   4014,   4041,   4410
    (b) 2211,   1112,   2111,   2121

5. Find the product of 125 and 8.

6. Find the quotient and remainder when 500 is divided by 8.

7. What number must be subtracted from 55 to give the answer 44?

8. (a) How many $10 notes can you get for $200?
    (b) How many 5¢ coins can you get for $1.50?

9. Find the missing numerator or denominator.

    (a) $\dfrac{1}{4} = \dfrac{\blacksquare}{12}$ (b) $\dfrac{2}{3} = \dfrac{6}{\blacksquare}$ (c) $\dfrac{8}{10} = \dfrac{4}{\blacksquare}$

10. Ring the smaller fraction.

    (a) $\dfrac{1}{3}$, $\dfrac{1}{4}$ (b) $\dfrac{2}{7}$, $\dfrac{4}{7}$ (c) $\dfrac{10}{10}$, $\dfrac{11}{12}$

    (d) $\dfrac{3}{6}$, $\dfrac{5}{8}$ (e) $\dfrac{2}{5}$, $\dfrac{3}{8}$ (f) $\dfrac{3}{7}$, $\dfrac{2}{5}$

11. Find the missing numbers.
    (a) 4 m 20 cm = ▮ cm   (b) 205 cm = ▮ m ▮ cm
    (c) 2 km 95 m = ▮ m   (d) 1600 m = ▮ km ▮ m
    (e) 1 kg 40 g = ▮ g   (f) 2450 g = ▮ kg ▮ g
    (g) 3 ℓ 60 ml = ▮ ml   (h) 2525 ml = ▮ ℓ ▮ ml

12. John bought 6 pears.
    He gave the cashier $5.
    How much change did he receive?

13. A badminton racket costs $9.60.
    A tennis racket costs $38.40.
    How much more is the cost of the tennis racket than the
    cost of the badminton racket?

14. The tub contains 1 litre of ice cream.
    Peter and his friends eat 325 ml of it.
    How much ice cream is left?

15. Sally bought 10 packets of milk.
    Each packet contained 125 ml of milk.
    Find the total amount of milk in litres and millilitres.

16. Muthu spent $\frac{4}{9}$ of his pocket money and saved the rest.
    What fraction of his pocket money did he save?

17. Minghua spent $\frac{3}{7}$ of his money on a book and the rest on a
    racket.
    What fraction of his money was spent on the racket?

7
Time

1 Hours and Minutes

David

8.20
20 minutes past 8

8.35
25 minutes to 9

David started running at 8.20 a.m.
He ran 3 km.
He finished at 8.35 a.m.
He took 15 minutes to run 3 km.

65

We read 8.20 as **eight twenty**. 8.20 is 20 minutes after 8 o'clock. We say the time is twenty minutes past eight.

We read 8.35 as **eight thirty-five**. 8.35 is 25 minutes before 9 o'clock. We say the time is twenty-five minutes to nine.

1. Find out how many times you can write your name in 1 minute.

2. What time is it?

(a)

(b)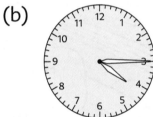

(c)

(d)

(e)

(f)

Workbook Exercise 36

3. What time is 26 minutes after 9.30 a.m.?

26 minutes later

4. How many minutes are there in **1 hour**?

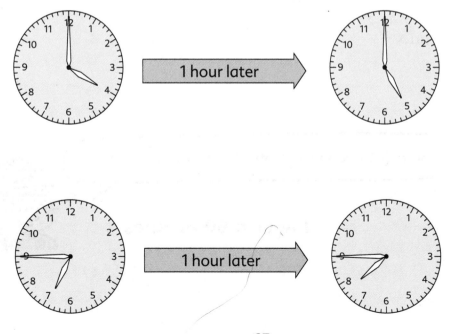

1 hour later

1 hour later

5. (a) How many **minutes** are there from 1.15 p.m. to 1.42 p.m.?

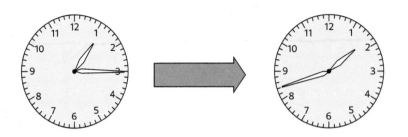

(b) How many **hours** are there from 3.18 p.m. to 8.18 p.m.?

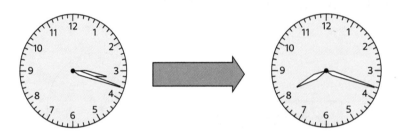

(c) How long is it from 9.15 a.m. to 11.30 a.m.?

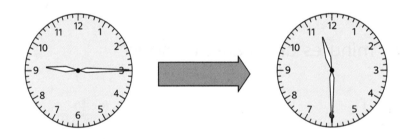

The **hour (h)** and **minute (min)** are units of time.

1 hour = 60 minutes

Workbook Exercise 37

6. The table shows the time taken by 3 children to paint a picture.

   (a) Who took the longest time?
   (b) Who took the shortest time?

Name	Time taken
Aihua	1 h 15 min
Jane	2 h 5 min
Siti	1 h 20 min

7. Mary took 1 h 35 min to complete a jigsaw puzzle.
   Write the time taken in minutes.

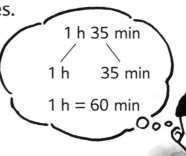

   1 h 35 min = ▮ min

8. Write in minutes.
   (a) 2 h   (b) 2 h 10 min   (c) 2 h 45 min
   (d) 3 h   (e) 3 h 5 min   (f) 3 h 15 min

9. Mrs Lin sewed 4 sets of curtains.
   She took 50 minutes to sew each set of curtains.
   Find the total time taken in hours and minutes.

   50 min × 4 = 200 min

   200 min = ▮ h ▮ min

10. Write in hours and minutes.
    (a) 70 min   (b) 85 min   (c) 100 min
    (d) 125 min   (e) 160 min   (f) 210 min

Workbook Exercise 38

11. A plane left Singapore at 8.00 a.m.
    It arrived in Penang at 9.05 a.m.
    How long did the journey take?

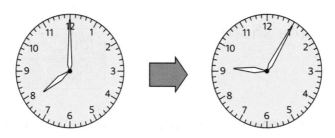

    The journey took ⬛ h ⬛ min.

12. Mrs Fu went to market at 7.15 a.m.
    She came home 1 h 45 min later.
    When did she come home?

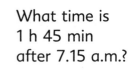

What time is
1 h 45 min
after 7.15 a.m.?

    She came home at ⬛ a.m.

13. Sally took 1 h 10 min to do her homework.
    She finished doing her homework at 9.40 p.m.
    When did she start?

What time is
1 h 10 min
before 9.40 p.m.?

    She started at ⬛ p.m.

Workbook Exercise 39

14.

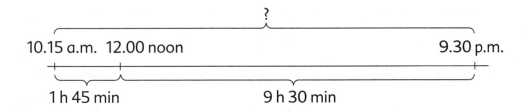

(a) 2.00 p.m. is ⬛ h after 12.00 noon.

(b) 3.30 p.m. is ⬛ h ⬛ min after 12.00 noon.

(c) 10.45 a.m. is ⬛ h ⬛ min before 12.00 noon.

15. A supermarket is open from 10.15 a.m. to 9.30 p.m. every day.
How long is the supermarket open a day?

1 h 45 min + 9 h 30 min = ⬛ h ⬛ min

The supermarket is open ⬛ h ⬛ min a day.

71

16.

9.10 p.m.   12.00 midnight   4.00 a.m.   6.40 a.m.

(a) 4.00 a.m. is ▆ h after 12.00 midnight.

(b) 6.40 a.m. is ▆ h ▆ min after 12.00 midnight.

(c) 9.10 p.m. is ▆ h ▆ min before 12.00 midnight.

17. A night tour began at 10.30 p.m. and lasted 3 h 20 min. When did the night tour end?

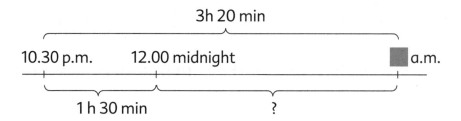

3 h 20 min

10.30 p.m.   12.00 midnight   ▆ a.m.

1 h 30 min   ?

$$3 \text{ h } 20 \text{ min} \xrightarrow{-1\text{ h}} 2 \text{ h } 20 \text{ min} \xrightarrow{-30\text{ min}} 1 \text{ h } 50 \text{ min}$$

3 h 20 min − 1 h 30 min = ▆ h ▆ min

The night tour ended at ▆ a.m.

18. Add or subtract.
(a) 2 h 40 min + 3 h   (b) 2 h 20 min + 45 min
(c) 3 h 15 min − 2 h   (d) 3 h 5 min − 30 min
(e) 1 h 25 min + 2 h 15 min (f) 2 h 40 min + 2 h 25 min
(g) 3 h 50 min − 1 h 35 min (h) 3 h 20 min − 1 h 40 min

Workbook Exercise 40

PRACTICE 7A

1. Add or subtract.
   (a) 1 h 45 min + 2 h   (b) 3 h 40 min − 2 h
   (c) 2 h 15 min + 45 min   (d) 3 h − 1 h 45 min
   (e) 1 h 30 min + 1 h 50 min   (f) 2 h 10 min − 1 h 30 min

2. This clock is 5 minutes slow.
   What is the correct time?

3. How long is it?
   (a) From 4.40 a.m. to 11.55 a.m.
   (b) From 5.45 p.m. to 7.00 p.m.
   (c) From 10.05 p.m. to 12.00 midnight
   (d) From 2.40 p.m. to 3.25 p.m.

4. Mr Chen took 2 h 35 min to repair a van and 1 h 55 min to repair a car.
   (a) How long did he take to repair both vehicles?
   (b) How much longer did he take to repair the van than the car?

5. Chandran took 2 h 30 min to paint his room.
   He began at 9.20 a.m.
   What time did he finish painting his room?

6. A group of children left for an excursion at 8.30 a.m.
   They returned 4 h 10 min later.
   What time did they return?

7. A supermarket opens for business at 9.30 a.m.
   Its workers have to report for work 40 minutes earlier.
   What time must the workers report for work?

② Other Units of Time

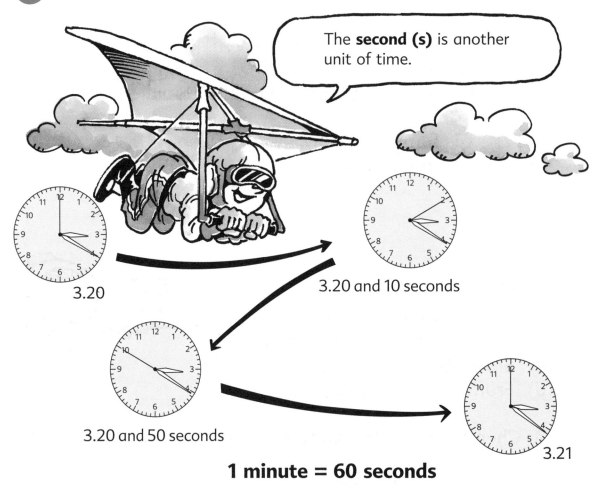

The **second (s)** is another unit of time.

3.20

3.20 and 10 seconds

3.20 and 50 seconds

3.21

1 minute = 60 seconds

1. (a) Find out how many times you can skip in 10 seconds.

   (b) How long do you take to write the word SINGAPORE?
   (c) How long do you take to run 100 m?

Workbook Exercise 41

The hour (h), minute (min) and second (s) are units of time.

   1 h = 60 min
   1 min = 60 s

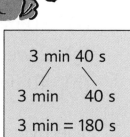

2. (a) Write 3 min 40 s in seconds.

   3 min 40 s = ▢ s

> 3 min 40 s
> ╱   ╲
> 3 min   40 s
>
> 3 min = 180 s

(b) Write 150 s in minutes and seconds.

   150 s = ▢ min ▢ s

> 150 s
> ╱   ╲
> 120 s   30 s
>
> 120 s = 2 min

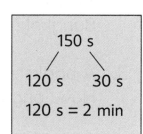

> Workbook Exercise 42

The year, month, week and day are units of time too.

3. (a) 1 year = ▢ months
   (b) 2 years = ▢ months
   (c) 2 years 4 months = ▢ months
   (d) 40 months = ▢ years ▢ months

4. (a) 1 week = ▢ days
   (b) 3 weeks = ▢ days
   (c) 3 weeks 4 days = ▢ days
   (d) 30 days = ▢ weeks ▢ days

> Workbook Exercises 43 & 44

75

PRACTICE 7B

1. Find the missing numbers.

   (a) 2 h 12 min = ■ min   (b) 108 min = ■ h ■ min

   (c) 2 min 3 s = ■ s   (d) 94 s = ■ min ■ s

   (e) 1 year 9 months = ■ months

   (f) 30 months = ■ years ■ months

   (g) 2 weeks 5 days = ■ days

   (h) 40 days = ■ weeks ■ days

2. The flying time from Singapore to Bangkok is 1 h 35 min
   and from Singapore to Manila is 3 h 15 min.
   How much longer does it take to fly to Manila than to
   Bangkok?

3. A bookshop is open from 9.30 a.m. to 5.00 p.m.
   How long is the bookshop open?

4. Mrs Ma went shopping at 10.20 a.m.
   She returned home 4 hours later.
   When did she return home?

5. Devi completed a jigsaw puzzle in 1 h 6 min.
   Lily completed the same jigsaw puzzle 10 minutes faster.
   How long did Lily take to complete the jigsaw puzzle?

6. Mr Li and his family went to Changi Beach for a picnic.
   They left home at 8.30 a.m. and arrived at Changi Beach at
   9.15 a.m.
   How long did the journey take?

7. Mr Chen took 8 h 45 min to drive from Singapore to
   Kuala Lumpur.
   He arrived there at 2.15 p.m.
   What time did he leave Singapore?

REVIEW E

1. What time is it?
   (a) 8 h 55 min after 12.00 noon
   (b) 1 h 30 min after 12.00 midnight

2. Write the missing numerator or denominator.

   (a)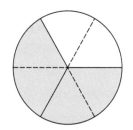

   $$\frac{2}{3} = \frac{\blacksquare}{6}$$

   (b)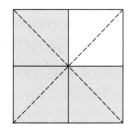

   $$\frac{3}{4} = \frac{6}{\blacksquare}$$

   (c)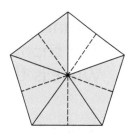

   $$\frac{4}{5} = \frac{\blacksquare}{10}$$

3. This graph shows the number of vehicles in a car park.

   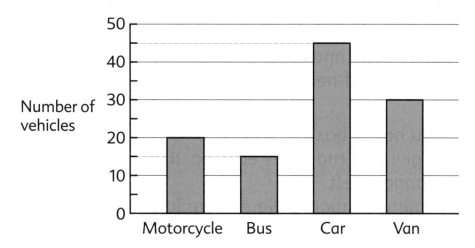

   (a) How many more vans than buses were there?
   (b) If there were 90 parking lots for cars and vans, how many of them were **not** occupied?

4. Mr Chen stayed in Japan for 19 months.
   Mr Lin stayed there for 2 years 4 months.
   Who stayed longer?
   How many months longer?

5. A machine can fill 140 jars of jam in 10 minutes.
   How many jars can it fill in 1 minute?

6. An art lesson started at 5.40 p.m.
   It lasted 45 minutes.
   When did the lesson end?

7. A tank can hold 10 times as much water as a pail.
   The capacity of the tank is 60 litres.
   What is the capacity of the pail?

8. A piece of ribbon 1 m long is cut into two pieces.

   One piece is $\frac{5}{8}$ m long.

   What is the length of the other piece?

9. Mr Fu bought a toothbrush and a tube of toothpaste.
   A toothbrush cost $6.50.
   A tube of toothpaste cost $1.80.
   How much did he pay altogether?

10. Mr Wu had a box of mangoes.
    After giving 3 mangoes each to 16 children, he had
    20 mangoes left.
    How many mangoes were there in the box at first?

11. Fatimah spent $4.80 on strings and $2.50 on beads to
    make a flowerpot hanger.
    How much did it cost her to make a flowerpot hanger?

12. Mrs Chen bought 8 towels.
    She gave the cashier $50 and received $2 change.
    (a) How much did she pay for the towels?
    (b) What was the cost of 1 towel?

Geometry

1 Angles

Use two cards to form an **angle** like this:

Then make a bigger angle.
What is the biggest angle you can get?
Compare it with your friends'.

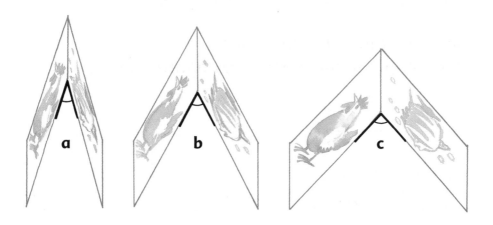

Which angle is the smallest?
Which angle is the biggest?

1. Here are some examples of angles.

Look for some more angles around you.

2. Two sides of a triangle make an angle.

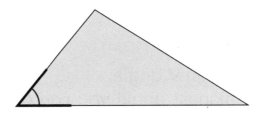

A triangle has ▇ sides and ▇ angles.

3. Here are some 4-sided figures.
    How many angles does each figure have?

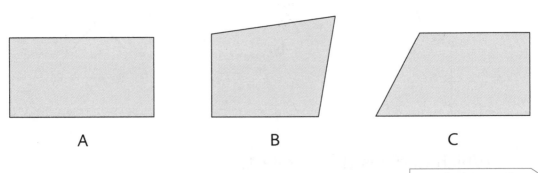

A   B   C

Workbook Exercise 45

② Right Angles

Fold a piece of paper twice to make an angle like this:

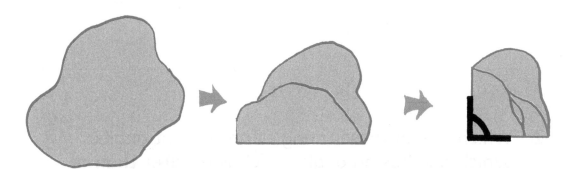

The angle you have made is a special one.
It is a **right angle**.
Use the right angle you have made to find out which of
the following angles are right angles.

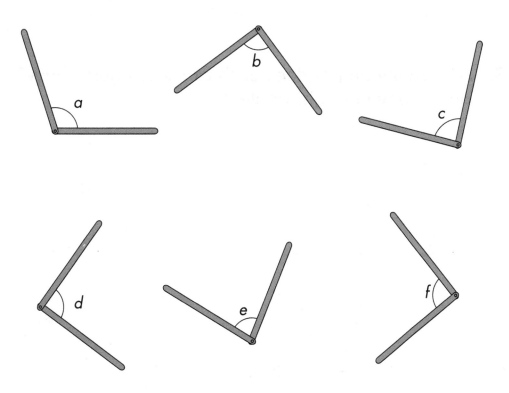

Use the right angle you have made to look for right angles
around you.

1. How many right angles can you find in
   (a) a square   (b) a rectangle?

2. Which one of these triangles has a right angle?
   Which one has an angle which is **greater than** a
   right angle?

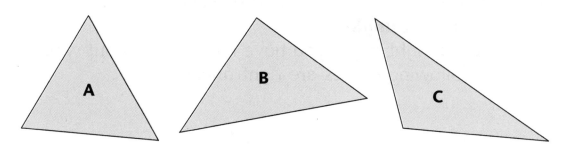

3. How many angles does each of these figures have?
   How many are right angles?

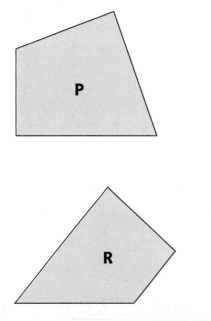   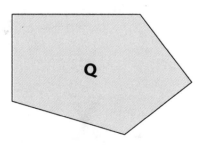

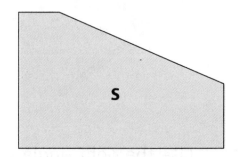

Workbook Exercise 46

Area and Perimeter

1 Area

Make 4 square cards and 4 half-square cards.

Use the cards to make different figures like these:

Each ⬜ is 1 square unit.

Each ◺ is $\frac{1}{2}$ square unit.

The figures have the same **area**.
The area of each figure is ▮ square units.

1. What is the area of each of the following figures?

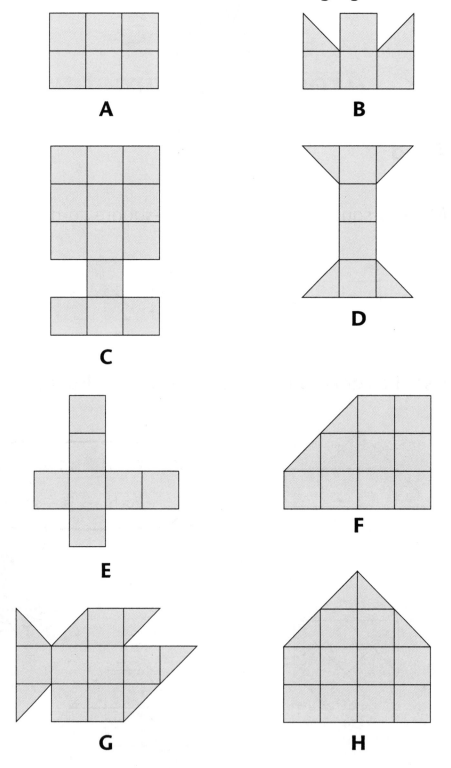

A

B

C

D

E

F

G

H

Which figure has the smallest area?
Which figure has the greatest area?

Workbook Exercise 47

2. This is a 1-cm square.

1 cm
1 cm

Each side of the square is 1 cm long.

Its area is 1 **square centimetre (cm²)**.

Give the area of each of the following squares in square centimetres.

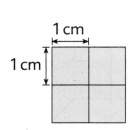
1 cm
1 cm

a 2-cm square

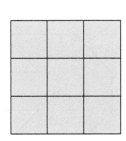

a 3-cm square

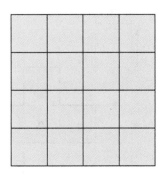

a 4-cm square

The square centimetre (cm²) is a unit of area.

A 2-cm square is made up of 4 pieces of 1-cm squares. Its area is 4 cm².

3. (a) What is the area of a 5-cm square?
   (b) What is the area of a 10-cm square?

4. This figure is made up of 1-cm squares.
   Find its area.

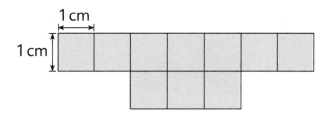

5. What is the area of each of the following figures?

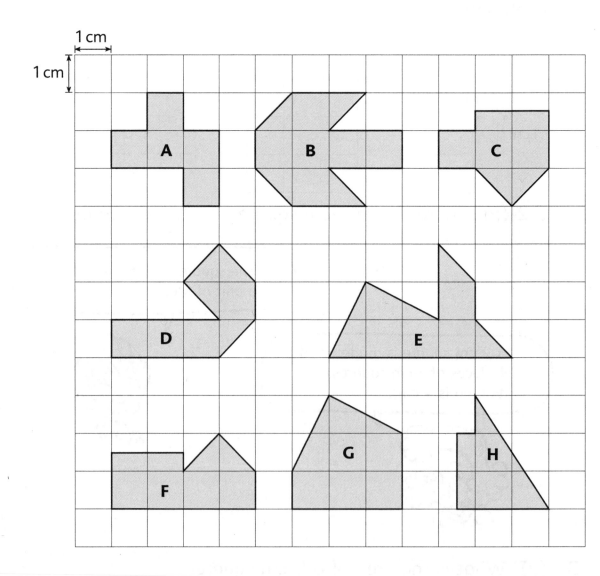

Workbook Exercise 48

6. Each side of this square is 1 m long.

Its area is 1 **square metre (m²)**.

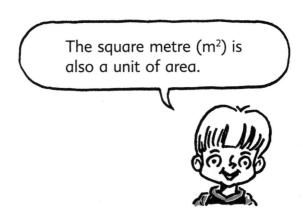

The square metre (m²) is also a unit of area.

Give the area of each of the following figures in square metres.

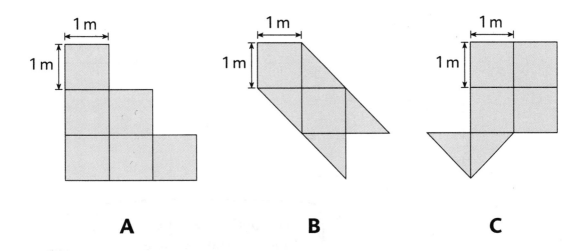

A   B   C

Which figure has the greatest area?
Which figure has the smallest area?

Workbook Exercise 49

2 Perimeter

Sumei used 3 pieces of wire of the same length to make the triangle, the square and the rectangle.

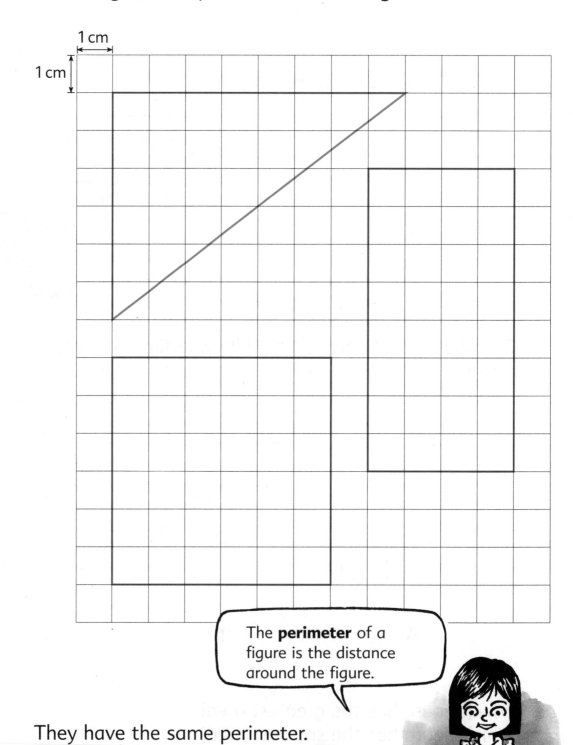

The **perimeter** of a figure is the distance around the figure.

They have the same perimeter.
The perimeter of each figure is ■ cm.

1. Measure with thread, the perimeter of each of these figures.

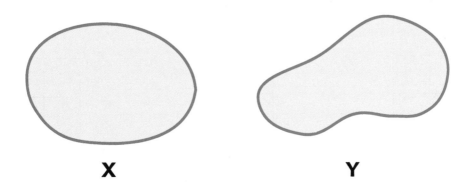

X   **Y**

Which figure has a longer perimeter?

2. (a) Measure the perimeter of your textbook in centimetres.
   (b) Measure the perimeter of your classroom in metres.

3. These two figures are made up of the same number of 1-cm squares.

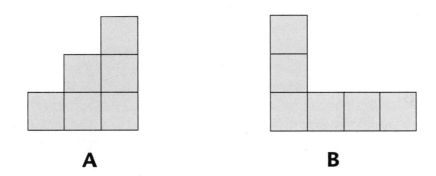

A   **B**

(a) They have the same area.
   The area of each figure is ▨ cm².

(b) They have different perimeters.
   The perimeter of Figure A is ▨ cm.
   The perimeter of Figure B is ▨ cm.

4. These figures are made up of 1-cm squares.

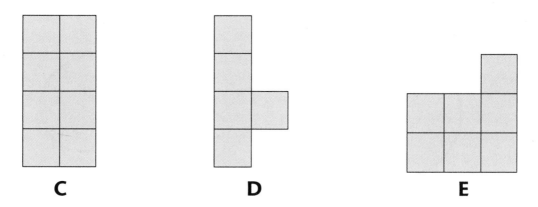

C   D   E

(a) Do they have the same area?
(b) Do they have the same perimeter?

5. These figures are made up of 1-cm squares.

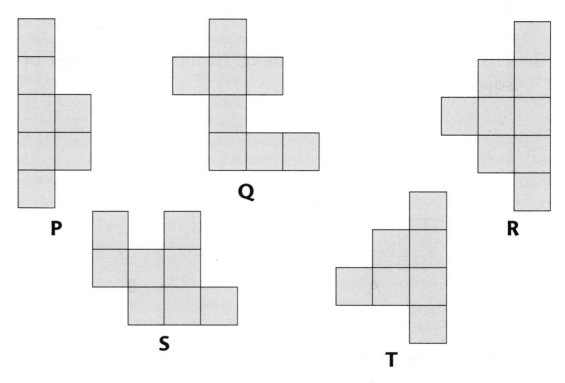

P   Q   R   S   T

(a) Which two figures have the same area but different perimeters?
(b) Which two figures have the same perimeter but different areas?
(c) Which two figures have the same area and perimeter?

6. (a) Each side of the square is 6 cm long.
Find its perimeter.

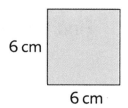

Perimeter = 6 + 6 + 6 + 6

= ▉ cm

(b) The length of the rectangle is 12 cm.
Its breadth is 4 cm.
Find its perimeter.

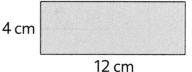

Perimeter = 12 + 4 + 12 + 4

= ▉ cm

7. Find the perimeter of each of the following figures:

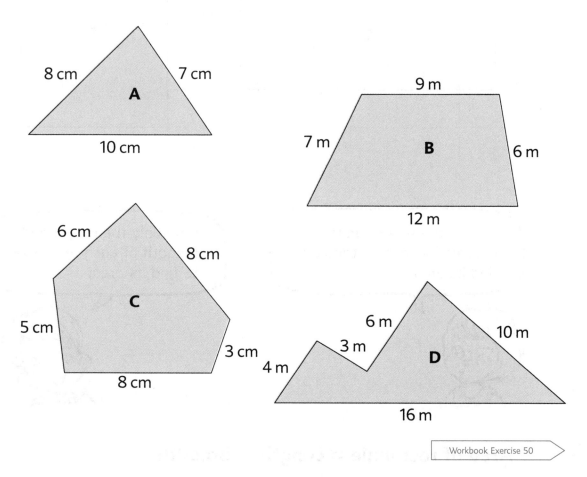

91

3 Area of a Rectangle

Find the area of each of the following rectangles:

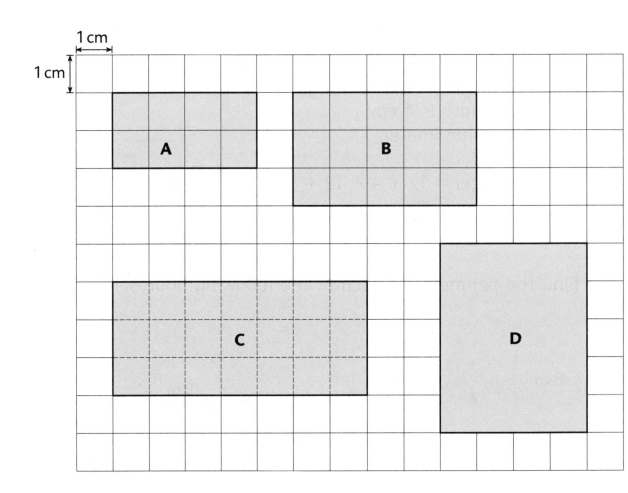

I count the square units covered by each rectangle to find its area.

I multiply the length and breadth of each rectangle to find its area.

Area of rectangle = Length × Breadth

1. Find the area of the rectangle.

Area of rectangle
= 5 × 4
= 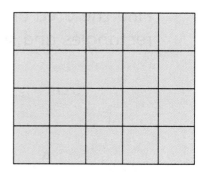 square units

2. Find the area of each of the following rectangles:

(a)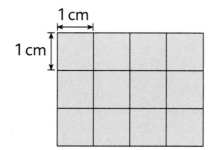

(b)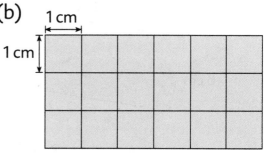

(c)

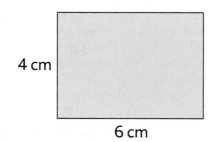

4 cm

6 cm

(d)

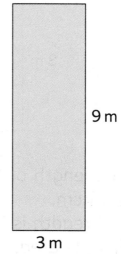

9 m

3 m

(e)

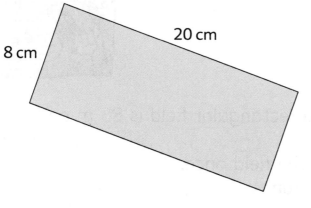

20 cm

8 cm

Workbook Exercises 51 & 52

PRACTICE 9A

1. Find the area and the perimeter of each of the following rectangles and squares:

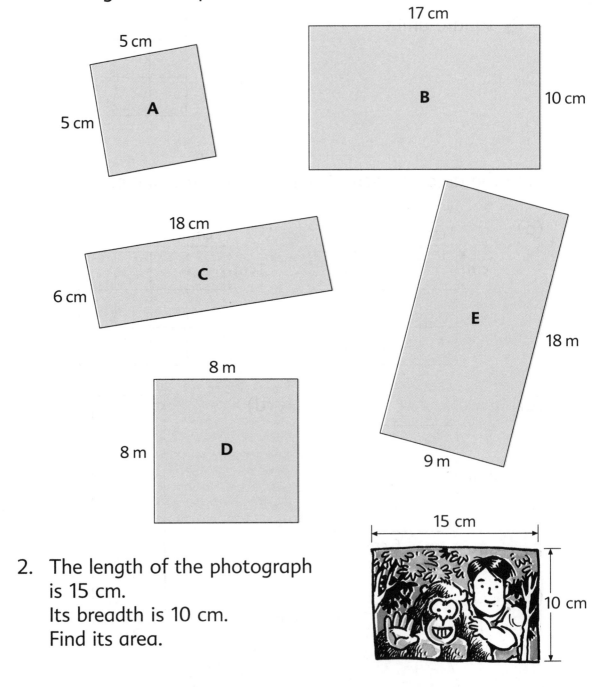

2. The length of the photograph is 15 cm.
   Its breadth is 10 cm.
   Find its area.

3. The length of a rectangular field is 85 m and its breadth is 10 m.
   Ali ran around the field once.
   How far did he run?

REVIEW F

1. Arrange the fractions in order, beginning with the smallest.

   (a) $\dfrac{3}{4}$, $\dfrac{1}{2}$, $\dfrac{5}{8}$　　　　　　(b) $\dfrac{1}{2}$, $\dfrac{3}{5}$, $\dfrac{3}{10}$

2. Each side of a triangle is 9 cm long.
   Find the perimeter of the triangle.

3. This graph shows the heights of the pupils in Mrs Lin's class.

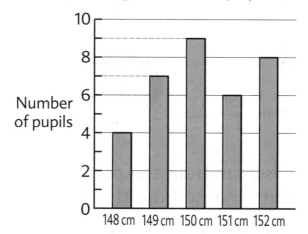

   Study the graph and answer these questions.
   (a) How many pupils are 150 cm tall?
   (b) How many pupils are taller than 150 cm?
   (c) How many pupils are in the tallest group?

4. Tom bought a wire and cut it into 8 pieces.
   Each piece of wire was 30 cm long.
   Find the length of the wire he bought.
   Give the answer in metres and centimetres.

5. 2500 people took part in a civil defence exercise.
   1360 of them were men.
   240 were children.
   The rest were women.
   (a) How many women were there?
   (b) How many more adults than children were there?

6. Mrs Chen made 286 cookies.
She gave away 30 cookies and sold the rest at 8 for $1.
How much money did she receive?

7. Each side of a square is 6 cm long.
Find the area of the square.

8. Anna, Peter and John shared a pizza.

Anna and Peter each received $\frac{1}{5}$ of the pizza.

What fraction of the pizza did John receive?

9.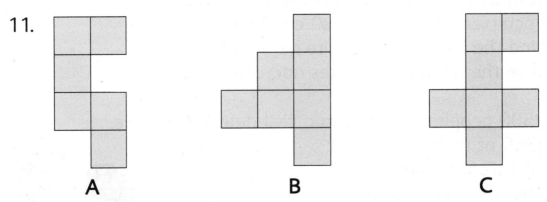

580 m

Park

Library

?

Tom's house

Tom's house is 1 km from the park.
How far is Tom's house from the library?

10. (a) What is the total weight of the
3 pieces of butter and the
packet of flour?
(b) If each piece of butter weighs
300 g, find the weight of the packet
of flour in kilograms and grams.

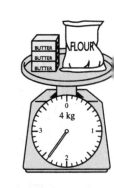

11.

A

B

C

(a) Which two figures have the same area?
(b) Which two figures have the same perimeter?